Prayers of Sorrow and Devotion

kevin mayhew

Out of the depths of life's torrents
I make a prayer of stillness
and plunge into God's holy presence.

Afloat in an ocean of need
I make a prayer of direction
and steer towards God's port.

God of the storm, God of the stillness,
of squalls of power and of shimmering calm,
into life's troughs and into life's billows
come with the reach of your long right arm.

Grant my head the waters of lament
and my ears the tears of sorrow.
The beautiful stones of the nature you have given me
have become defaced.
The precious robe of chastity has been torn.
Devotions of love have been scattered,
inspirations have been squandered.

Dear Father,
you know how I long for you.
Show your favour to me.
Snatch me from the wastelands,
restore to me a place in your royal commonwealth.
Fill me once again with your Holy Spirit.
Heal my wounds
and I will love you, dwell with you and serve you for ever.

Inspired by words of Moucan, British eighth century or earlier.

Pain-bearer and Love-maker,
steep our souls in your deeps
that we may walk with Christ
through the pain to the glory.

We confess deeds of wrong
which cause ills to fester still;
the loss in the Church of integrity, humility and patience,
the crushing of spontaneity,
the caging of the wild Spirit,
the breaking off of relationships,
the bruising of the crushed reeds,
the arrogance of the intellect.

Give us hearts of sorrow for all that spoils your people.
Give us hearts of sorrow for all that spoils your land.

We are the race that helped cut the wood
on which you were crucified,
and still we misuse your creation.

We are the race that helped make the nails
that pierced your body,
yet still we use work for gain at others' expense.

We are the race that did nothing to stop your betrayers,
yet still we are ruled by comfort or cowardice.

Draw us to the place of at-one-ment:
give us tears to see the wonder of your presence;
give us tears to see the wasting of your people,
give us tears to see the wounding of your Son.

O Saviour of the human race,
O true physician of every disease,
O heart-pitier and assister of all misery,
O fount of true purity and true knowledge:
Forgive.

O star-like sun
O guiding light
O home of the planets
O fiery-maned and marvellous one:
Forgive.

O holy scholar of holy strength.
O overflowing, loving, silent one.
O generous and thunderous giver of gifts.
O rock-like warrior of a hundred hosts:
Forgive.

Attributed to Ciaran.

Eternal God who mothers us all,
sinners find mercy in you and saints find joy.
You hold all souls in life;
the dead as well as the living are in your care.
Thank you for the wonder and variety of human lives.
Today we remember in your presence those who died
frustrated in their hopes,
disappointed in themselves,
unrewarded by others.
We remember forgotten souls
whose names are known to you alone
and those cut down in prime of life.

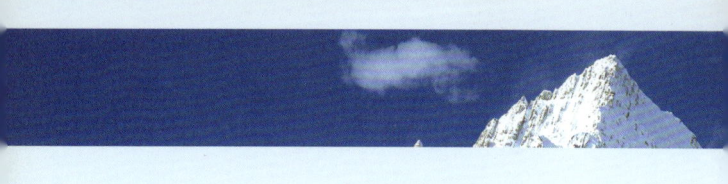

Eternal God, we honour
the wondrous gift of life,
the awesome gift of choice,
the immense gift of possibility, for good or ill,
which you have given to your human family.

Eternal God, we mourn
for the goodness and wisdom that perished with
those who died,
for the skill and wit, the learning,
the laughter and leadership that were lost.
The world has become a poorer place and our hearts
become cold
as we think of the splendour that might have been.
Like candles in the night, they shone and flickered out.
Lord God, be with us yet, lest we forget.

Heal the ancient wound that festers in humanity's heart.
Salvage hope from the wrecks of time.
May compassion grow in places where much blood
has been shed.
Come to those who suffer pain and injustice.
Heal those who can barely live with memories
of injury or loss.
Holy Jesus, grant rest eternal
to those who were snatched from earth by violent death.
Holy Jesus, grant rest eternal
to those whose sleep is stolen by the ravages of memory
Holy Jesus, grant rest eternal.

Forgive us for the places in our lives
where fear has driven out love.

Forgive us for the places in our lives
where fear has frozen out action.

Forgive us for the places in our lives where
fear has dried up creativity.

Sorry, Lord,
for shabby living,
for shoddy working,
for hollow praying,
for selfish giving,
for fickle feeling,
for faithless speaking,
for dull hearing,
for grudging sharing,
for slothful thinking,
for slow serving,
for cold loving.

For ugly buildings
that violate the shape of the land
and the human soul's need for beauty,
we grieve with you, O Lord.

For the rainforests gone,
and the deserts caused by human destruction,
we grieve with you, O Lord.

For polluted seas,
dirty streets and litter,
we grieve with you, O Lord.

For demanding such variety of food and drink
that we neglect to have things in season,
we grieve with you, O Lord.

For not being content
to savour the simple gifts of creation,
we grieve with you, O Lord.

We offer to you all we are, all we have, all we do,
and all whom we shall meet this day,
that you will be given the glory.

We offer to you our homes, our work, our schools,
make them signs of your creation,
may all be done as unto you.

We offer to you the coal and oil,
the seas and soil, the air and animals;
may we steward your creation to your glory
and for the benefit of future generations.

Teach us, good God,
to enjoy the laughter in your creation
and not to take ourselves too seriously.

Teach us, good God,
to allow the sense of humour
which is your gift to us
to bubble over as it should.

May our girls have the beauty of serenity.
May our boys have the strength of loyalty.

May the voice of complaining cease from our streets.
May the goods we buy make for well-being.

May we make no distinction between rich and poor.
May we treat each person as a royal soul.

May love in our hearts be stronger than fear.
May belief in good be stronger than sloth.

Take my hands, Lord,
let them be
to the world
a touch from thee.

To the folk out in the cold
may they circle and enfold.

To the weary and worn through
may they lift and make them new.

To the orphaned and alone
may they for their lack atone.

Take my hands, Lord,
let them be
to the world
a touch from thee.

God of the hills, God of the outposts,
go before us now.

God of the streets, God of the gutters,
go before us now.

God of the parties, God of the pains,
go before us now.

God of achievements, God of failures,
go before us now.

God of beginnings, God of endings,
go before us now.

Help us to keep always before us, O God,
the fleeting nature of this life,
and the eternal community for which we are destined.

Help us to keep always far from us, O God,
ill-will towards others,
and misuse of time and talents.

Help us to keep always before us, O God,
the racecourse you have chosen for us,
and Jesus, from its start to its finish.

May I grow a little today, dear God,
in goodness and greatness of spirit.

May I grow a little today, dear God,
in wisdom and discernment of spirit.

May I grow a little today, dear God,
in kindness and out-going of spirit.

Jesus, you stopped the wind.
Jesus, you stilled the waves.
Bring calm to us today.

Jesus, of purest love.
Jesus, the perfect friend.
Bring warmth to us today.

Jesus, of lakeside meal.
Jesus, the Bread of life.
Bring us ashore today.

Open our eyes to your Presence.
Open our ears to your call.
Open our hearts to your mercies.
That you be our all in all.

Forgive our sins of omission.
Our pride and each thoughtless way.
Forgive our sins of commission,
the words that lead others astray.

Take from us our sloth and dullness,
all spirit of blame and despair.
Give to us eyes for fresh ventures,
help us to soar through the air.

We give thanks for the Christian family,
for the marvellous ways you have led,
we give thanks that your hand will guide us,
to good challenges further ahead.

Give us this day your wisdom
and love for one and all.
Help us to learn to listen
and together respond to your call.

Eternal Source,

may the gods that fail us wither.

Help us to touch you in the deep places of the world.

In empty souls,

in teeming thought,

in aching hearts,

in wasted lands.

Great Spirit,
may we see you
in the glowing of a fire,
and the flowing of a tide,
in the beauty of a dawn,
and the brooding of a dusk,
in the caring of a friend,
and the harvest of long toil.

I light this candle.
Let it be a light to illumine the darkest maze.
Let it be a fire to burn out selfish traits.
Let it be a flame to warm the coldest days.
Let it be a sign to brighten shadowed ways.

Transform our jaded routines.
Heal our wounded lives.
Revive our thirsting souls.
Restore our fading sight.

As the sun circles the world,
circle this land, O God,
circle the soil, circle the waters,
circle the crops, circle the homes.
Keep harm without, keep good within.

Light up the people with your Light.
Light up creation with your Life.
Light up the Church with your Lamb.
Light up our tables with your Fare.

Cherished be the earth, Lord,
in this place.

Cradled be the Faith, Lord,
in this place.

Flowing be the life, Lord,
in this place.

Holy be the folk, Lord,
in this place.

I give thanks for the gift of night
and the gift of this new day.
I give thanks for the gift of life,
for health and the bright sun's ray.

I pray for those wracked in pain,
for whom the day seems night.
May they know that every soul
is being birthed for heaven's sight.

Like members of one body,
may the strong send strength to the weak.
Like sharers of one chalice,
may the frail receive from the sleek.

The Creator give you a single eye
that you may see like an eagle.
The Saviour give you a hospitable heart
that others may warm themselves there.
The Spirit give you the weaver's art,
that will help you to restore the broken strands.
The Three with the saints of heaven go with you
and inspire you to join them in the adventure without end.

May we be
immersed in the greatness of the Father,
buried in the depths of the Son,
borne along in the flowing of the Spirit.

For your love for us, wild and freeing,
which has awakened us to your pulse in nature
and in human life,
we honour you and give you our love.

For your love for us, suffering and patient,
which has brought us through pain, wept for us in
our sins,
and waited for us in our confusion,
we honour you and give you our love.

For your love for us, strong and challenging,
which has called us to risk all for you,
drawn out the best in us and shown us how to live,
we honour you and give you our love.

In the name of the creating Father,
in the name of the workaday Son,
in the name of the renewing Spirit,
in the name of the Three-In-One.

In the name of the dancing Father,
in the name of the rising Son,
in the name of the life-giving Spirit,
in the name of life we are one.

In the name of the Father who fosters,
in the name of the Son who sets free,
in the name of the Spirit who freshens,
in the name of the Sacred Three.

In the name of the God of thunder,
in the name of the Saviour from harm,
in the name of the Spirit of mercy,
we are safe in God's strong arm.

In the name of the sending Father,
in the name of the pilgrim Son,
in the name of the blowing Spirit,
in the name of the Three-in-One.

Here be the peace of those who do your sacred will.
Here be the praise of God by night and day.
Here be the place where strong ones serve the weakest.
Here be a sight of Christ's most gentle way.

Here be the strength of prophets righting greed
and wrong.
Here be the green of land that's tilled with love.
Here be the soil of holy lives maturing.
Here be a people one with all the saints above.

Echoes Aidan's Prayer for the English.

Praying and praising, immersed in your sea of love,
arms stretched like the Saviour's,
cross-like in mercy,
immersed in compassion,
Servant Christ,
help us to follow you deep into the waters of baptism.
Help us to follow you into the desert
where we are stripped of the surfeits that distract.
Help us to follow you into your work of healing
the world.

Into the life of the Father I immerse you
that he may protect you from harm,
bring you peace and calm.
Into the boundless life of your Maker I immerse you.

Into the life of the Son I immerse you
that he may save you from hell,
keep you washed and well.
Into the sinless life of your Saviour I immerse you.

Into the life of the Spirit I immerse you
that (s)he may light up your night,
give you power to do right.
Into the endless life of your Guide I immerse you.

Into the life of the Three I immerse you
that they may fill you with love,
lift you to heaven above.
Into the selfless love of the Trinity I immerse you.

The God of life be our champion and leader.
We shall not be left in the hand of the wicked,
we shall not be bent in the court of the false.
We shall rise victorious above them,
as rise victorious the crests of the waves.

Into the Sacred Three I immerse you.
Into their power and peace I place you.
May their breath be yours to live.
May their love be yours to give.

First published in 2005 by

KEVIN MAYHEW LTD
Buxhall, Stowmarket, Suffolk, IP14 3BW
E-mail: info@kevinmayhewltd.com
Website: www.kevinmayhew.com

© 2005 Ray Simpson

The right of Ray Simpson to be identified as the author of this work has been asserted by him in accordance with the Copyright, Designs and Patents Act, 1988.

No part of this publication may be reproduced, stored in a retrieval system, or transmitted, in any form or by any means, electronic, mechanical, photocopying, recording or otherwise, without the prior written permission of the publisher.

All rights reserved.

9 8 7 6 5 4 3 2 1 0

ISBN 1 84417 417 4
Catalogue No. 1500808

Designed by Chris Coe
Edited by Marian Reid

Printed and bound in China

Ray Simpson is a co-founder of the worldwide Community of Aidan and Hilda and is its first guardian. He lives on Lindisfarne, where the Community has a retreat and guesthouse: The Open Gate, Holy Island, Berwick-upon-Tweed, TD15 2SD.
The Community's website is www.aidan.org.uk